UXBRIDGE College Learning Centre
Coldharbour Lane, Hayes, Middlesex UB3 3BB
Telephone: 01895 853740

Please return this item to the Learning Centre
on or before the last date stamped below:

UXBRIDGE
COLLEGE

0 7 JAN 2004		
3 0 JAN 2006		
2 3 FEB 2006		
2 6 FEB 2007		
2 1 FEB 2022		
2 8 MAR 2022		
2 4 JUN 2022		
2 2 FEB 2024		
1 4 MAR 2024		362.734

LEARNING RESOURCES AT UXBRIDGE COLLEGE

Text copyright © Pat Thomas 2003
Illustrations copyright © Lesley Harker 2003

Editor: Liz Gogerly
Concept design: Kate Buxton
Design: Jean Scott-Moncrieff

Published in Great Britain in 2003 by Hodder Wayland,
an imprint of Hodder Children's Books

British Library Cataloguing in Publication Data

Thomas, Pat, 1959-
My parents picked me! : a first look at
adoption
1.Adoption - Juvenile literature
I.Title II.Harker, Lesley
362.7'34

ISBN 0 7502 4266 3

Printed in Hong Kong by Wing King Tong

Hodder Children's Books
A division of Hodder Headline Limited
338 Euston Road
London NW1 3BH

My Parents Picked Me!

A FIRST LOOK AT ADOPTION

PAT THOMAS
ILLUSTRATED BY LESLEY HARKER

HODDER
Wayland

An imprint of Hodder Children's Books

You live in a very
special family.

Out of all the children in the world, your parents chose you to be a part of their family.

There are lots of ways to make a family.

Sometimes children live with their birth parents –
the ones who gave birth to them.

Sometimes they live with relatives or other people who are not their parents.

And, sometimes children are adopted into a completely new family.

What about you?

Can you think of lots of different ways to make a family? What is the most important thing that families share?

We all have birth parents.

But sometimes our birth parents can not look after us as well as they would like to.

When this happens a child
sometimes goes to live with
a foster family or stays
in a children's home.

11

A foster family or a children's home usually
only looks after a child for a little while,
until their parents are able to take care
of them again.

But sometimes parents just can not look after their children.

When this happens a child stays with a foster family until a new family can be found. This new family is their adoptive family.

13

Every year lots of children all over the world are adopted –
sometimes as babies, and sometimes as older children.

When a child is adopted they go to live with
another family forever.

Adopting a child is not always easy. Grown-ups who want to adopt often have to answer a lot of questions about who they are and how they live.

Sometimes parents and children have to wait a long time before they can be part of a new family.

When your adoptive parents first saw
you they knew you were meant to be
a part of their family.

When they were finally able to adopt you they made a promise to love you and take care of you. They looked forward to watching you grow and teaching you new things.

Sometimes adopted children look like the members of their new family. Sometimes they may come from a different part of the country, or another part of the world.

But the way we look and where we come from
are not the most important things in a family.
What is important is sharing some of the same
interests and learning to understand and love
each other whatever happens.

Some children who are
adopted think they are
different or second best –
even though this is
not true.

They can also feel confused
or angry about not knowing
much about their birth
parents.

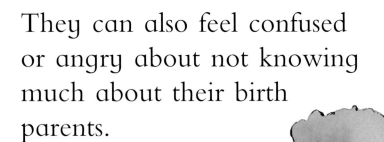

This is normal and your parents understand this. Talking to them about how you are feeling can help to make the hurt feelings go away.

Sometimes it can make you feel sad when
you think about your birth parents.
You might not understand why they
had you adopted.

Sometimes adoptive parents do not know much about your birth parents. Whatever they know they will try to share with you when they can.

What about you?

What do your adoptive parents know about your birth parents?
Is there anything that you would like to know?
Can your parents help you to find out more?
Look at pages 28-29.

Remember also that both of your sets of parents have given you something special. Your birth parents gave you life.

Your adoptive parents gave you a home and family and the love you need to grow up healthy and happy.

There are many different kinds of families. But there are some things that make all families the same.

Like the way they always try to love and support one another — just like everyone in your family does.

HOW TO USE THIS BOOK

Many adoptive parents agonize over the question, 'What do we tell the children?' What to say and when to say it are difficult questions to answer. Much depends on your child's age, sensitivity and level of understanding. It is generally accepted that children should know they are adopted even before they fully understand what it means. As soon as possible, initiate conversations about adoption. Try to make talk about adoption a part of normal everyday conversation. For example: 'Before we adopted you we lived in Manchester, now we live in London'. Casually dropping the subject in the conversation like this lets your child know that it is OK to talk about it when they want to. If adoption becomes part of the language of the family, it will not seem like such a big deal when the time comes to discuss it in depth.

Before you begin to talk to your child about adoption, practise what you want to say. Make sure you are prepared to answer any questions that come up. Books like this are helpful for getting a discussion going and are supposed to be read more than once.

Give yourself some credit. Adopting a child is a major life journey. Adoptive parents sometimes suffer from 'super parent' syndrome. They may feel that they have something to prove to others about how competent they are. Try to let this go because it gets in the way of open communication. You have come far enough to want to talk to your child about it. Let your loving feelings for your child be your guide about the best way to do this.

Talk to your children about all the different types of family. There are divorced families that include step-parents and siblings. Some children live with relatives other than their parents and foster families. Schools can make a similar effort. Whether there are adopted children in the class or not, discussions about family should always include information on different types of families so that all the children understand that there is nothing 'wrong' with being adopted.

Children love to hear their own stories. Very young children may only want to know pieces of the story, for instance how you came to get them the day they were adopted. As they get older they will ask more questions. Create an environment where it's OK for your child to ask questions. Keep all the information you have on your child's background in a safe place. When the time comes it will make it easier to answer questions.

Many parents put together a book for their adopted children. They collect pictures and stories which their child can add to later. Make your child's 'life story book' using whatever you have – pictures of your family and of the birth family if available. Other ideas might be photographs of previous homes or pets. If information is lacking (perhaps as a result of a closed adoption) you must do what you can with what you've got so your child has something to build on.

There are many myths about adoption which linger from the past. Though the adoption process has changed a great deal in the past twenty years, adoption can still be presented in a negative way. We still hear comments like: 'Your parents didn't want you' or 'We couldn't have any children of our own'. Similarly it is easy for adopted children to feel they are somehow 'second best'. In this book the author has attempted to introduce the subject from a more positive angle, and encourages parents to avoid making children feel grateful for being adopted.

Reassure your child that they didn't do anything wrong, and the break-up of their birth family was not their fault. Adoption is usually an act of love on the part of a birth parent. Help your child to understand the impossible position in which their parents might have been when they had them adopted. Stress that adoption seemed the only way that their birth parents thought they could help them. By having their child adopted, they believed that they were giving them the best opportunity for a happy life with a loving family that could look after them properly. When stuck for an explanation always err on the side of love.

Acknowledge your child's feelings and answer all questions even if they are difficult. If you don't know the answer to a particular question say so.

Celebrate your child's adoption day as well as their birthday. This can be a celebration involving the whole family. Special adoption celebration cards are also now available.

Use your adoption agency. If necessary, they will give you advice and help you to seek out more background information about your adopted child.

GLOSSARY

adoption When a child goes to live with another family forever. When a child is adopted the adoptive parents have a legal responsibility to look after that child.

birth parents The people who created you with their bodies and helped give you life.

foster family A family who looks after a child for a short while, for instance when the child's birth parents are very ill. When the birth parents are able to look after the child, he or she goes back to live with them.

FURTHER READING

Adoption is for Always
by Linda Walvoord Girard
(Albert Whitman & Co, 1991)

How I Was Adopted
by Joanna Cole (Morrow Junior Books, 1995)

Stuart Little
by EB White (Puffin, 2000)

The Mulberry Bird – An Adoption Story
by Anne Braff Brodzinsky (Perspectives Press, 1996)

What Do We Think About Adoption?
by Jillian Powell (Wayland, 1999)

Why Was I Adopted?
by Carole Livingson
(Angus and Robertson, 1978)

RESOURCES

Adoption UK
Manor Farm
Appletree Road
Chipping Warden
Banbury
Oxfordshire OX17 1LH
08707 700 450

Network that allows parents and children to share their experiences of adoption.

British Agency for Adoption and Fostering
Skyline House
Union St
London SE1 0LX
0207 593 2000

Information and advice for individuals, plus ongoing campaign to raise public awareness of adoption and fostering issues.

The Fostering Network
87 Blackfriars Road
London
SE1 8HA
020 7620 6400

A national charity providing advice, information and training on issues relating to young people and foster care.